Steck-Vaughn
Shutterbug Books
SOCIAL STUDIES

All Kinds of MUSEUMS

by Janet Reed Ahearn

Harcourt Achieve

Rigby • Saxon • Steck-Vaughn

www.HarcourtAchieve.com
1.800.531.5015

Contents

Metropolitan Museum of Art

Do you like to collect things? Do you keep your collection in a special place? Cities and countries collect things, too. They keep these treasures in museums.

Museums are places where people go to see and learn about many different things. There are many kinds of museums. Let's visit some of them!

Science Museums

Model helicopter in the Aviation Hall of Fame

Have you ever wondered why it rains or how airplanes fly? Science museums are great places to learn the answers to these kinds of questions. Science museums have **exhibits** that explain the world around us.

Model tornado in the Ontario Science Display

Many science museums have special **models** that help show how things work. You can pretend to fly a model helicopter or look closely at a model tornado. It would be too dangerous to watch a real tornado so closely!

Have you ever seen someone's hair stand on end? One science museum has a special machine that makes people's hair stand straight out. Most people call this machine the Hair Ball.

Girl touching the Hair Ball, a static electricity machine

Airplanes in the National Air and Space Museum

Another science museum tells all about flight. Visitors to this museum can learn how an airplane flies in the air. They can see many different kinds of airplanes. Some of the airplanes are new, and some are very old.

The Spirit of St. Louis in the National Air and Space Museum

At the same museum, there are many airplanes that have made history. One airplane was the very first to fly all the way across the Atlantic Ocean without stopping. This airplane is called the Spirit of St. Louis.

People can find other flying machines at this museum, too. They can even see a spacecraft that once landed on the moon. Visitors can see inside the spacecraft. They can see where the **astronauts** sat during the flight.

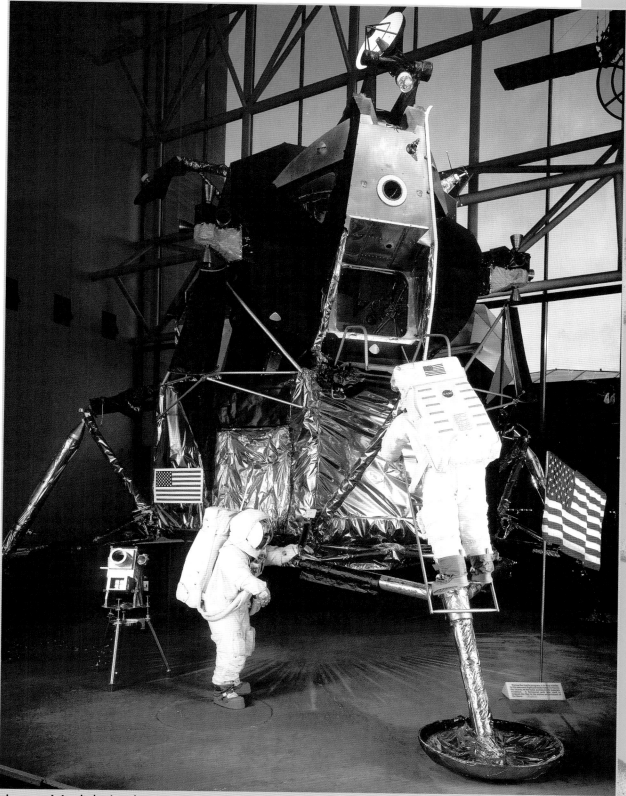

Lunar Module in the National Air and Space Museum

Model of the Universe in the Rose Center for Earth and Space

A **planetarium** is a special kind of science museum. It tells about the Earth and outer space. One planetarium has a huge model of the sun and planets in our solar system. The large ball in the center of the room is a model of the sun.

The model of the sun is so big that it has a theater inside. In this theater, you can learn about the night sky. You can see pictures of the stars on the curved ceiling. You can also see what planets and stars look like up close.

Natural History Museums

Dinosaur model in a natural history exhibit

Natural history museums tell about life today and life long ago. They have exhibits about people, plants, and animals from different places all over the world. These museums tell what life was like on Earth millions of years ago.

In a natural history museum, the dinosaur exhibits are often what people like the most. Dinosaurs lived over 200 million years ago, so you won't find them in the zoo. But you can see models of them in a museum.

Scientists find dinosaur bones in many places around the world. People work to put the dinosaur bones back together. Then they set them up in natural history museums for people to see.

Dinosaur skeletons in the American Museum of Natural History

African elephant in the National Museum of Natural History

Natural history museums show much more than just dinosaurs. At a natural history museum, you can see all kinds of wild animal models up close. Museum workers make models of animals and their homes. These models show just how big some animals really are!

History Museums

The Bob Bullock Texas State History Museum

Stagecoach in the National Museum of American History

History museums help people take a step back in time. These museums show how people lived long ago. They show the kinds of houses people lived in, the clothes they wore, and the kinds of tools that they used.

Some history museums show different kinds of **transportation** that people used long ago. Before there were cars, people traveled in other ways. Some people traveled in **stagecoaches** pulled by horses.

The Star Spangled Banner in the National Museum of American History

One history museum has one of the first American flags. "The Star Spangled Banner" is a song that was written about this very flag. This flag is almost 200 years old. How is it different from today's United States flag?

You can learn fun facts at a history museum, too. Did you know that the teddy bear was named for a United States President? It was named for President Teddy Roosevelt.

The first teddy bear in the National Museum of American History

19

Art Museums

The Mona Lisa by Leonardo da Vinci in the Louvre Museum

Art museums are filled with treasures. They show many different kinds of art that people have made. Many art museums show paintings. Some paintings, such as the Mona Lisa, are very famous. People all over the world recognize the face of the woman in this painting.

Paintings are only one of the many kinds of art you can find in a museum. You also can see photographs and **sculptures.** Some sculptures are carved out of stone. Others are made from clay or metal. The ballerina sculpture below is made out of metal and cloth.

Ballerina sculpture by Edgar Degas in the Metropolitan Museum of Art

Coffin of a mummy in the
Metropolitan Museum of Art

Tomb where mummies were buried

Ancient building in the Metropolitan Museum of Art

Some art museums show art made by people who lived thousands of years ago. Long ago in Egypt, many things were buried in rooms under the ground. Scientists found these rooms. They dug up the beautiful treasures.

These ancient treasures are now kept in art museums for many people to see. Some museums even have whole buildings inside! Visitors can walk around the ancient buildings just as people did thousands of years ago.

Children's Museums

Children listening to a Kwanzaa story at the Kohl Children's Museum

Children's museums are special museums. They have exhibits made just for children. At children's museums, you can learn about science, art, music, and more. Sometimes you can even sit and listen to a story!

At most museums, people are not allowed to touch the exhibits. But at children's museums, there are many things to touch. The children below are learning about turtles.

Children petting a turtle at the Dartmouth Children's Museum

"Map Your Head" exhibit at the Children's Discovery Museum of San José

Some children's museums have machines that make things. They make things you might not see every day. One children's museum has a machine that can take a picture of your whole head. Do you ever wonder what the back of your head looks like?

Giant bubble machine in the Louisiana Children's Museum

A machine at another museum makes giant bubbles. Would you like to stand inside a big bubble of soap? Other children's museums have classes where you can learn how to do things. You might learn how to paint a painting or build a sand castle.

ASTRONAUT

One-of-a-Kind Museums

Railroad engines in the California State Railroad Museum

Some museums only collect one kind of thing. Railroad museums only collect trains. At a railroad museum, you can learn about the history of trains. You can see how trains have changed over time by looking at different trains up close.

United States Astronaut Hall of Fame

Another kind of museum collects things that were used by famous people. There are museums about famous people in history, sports, movies, and music. This kind of museum is often called a **hall of fame.** The United States Astronaut Hall of Fame is all about astronauts.

Elvis Presley's clothes and guitars in the Rock and Roll Hall of Fame

The Rock and Roll Hall of Fame collects things that once belonged to famous musicians. It shows records, instruments, clothes, and other objects. Would you like to see a guitar that your favorite rock star played?

Outside a history museum at Ellis Island

People learn about all kinds of things at museums. They learn about science, history, art, and more. Each museum has its own special collection. Do you have a collection of something? Maybe someday you can open a museum of your own!

Glossary

astronauts	people who travel in space
exhibits	groups of objects shown in museums
hall of fame	a museum that collects objects from famous people
models	exact copies of things
natural history	the study of plants and animals from long ago
planetarium	a place to learn about the stars and planets
sculptures	art made from solid materials
stagecoaches	carriages, pulled by horses, which carried people from place to place
transportation	way of getting from one place to another